The Queen and her Family

By CJ Leonard

Senior Editor Cécile Landau
Project Editor Arpita Nath
Art Editor Kanika Kalra
Jacket Designer Amy Keast
Managing Editor Soma B. Chowdhury
Managing Art Editor Neha Ahuja Chowdhry
DTP Designers Syed Md Farhan, Dheeraj Singh
Picture Researchers Nishwan Rasool, Sakshi Saluja
Producer, Pre-production Dragana Puvacic
Senior Producer Srijana Gurung
Creative Director, Custom and Specials Helen Senior
Publisher Sarah Larter

First published in Great Britain by
Dorling Kindersley Limited
80 Strand, London, WC2R 0RL

A CIP catalogue record for this book
is available from the British Library.

ISBN: 978-0-2412-7895-6

Printed and bound in Slovakia.

The publisher would like to thank the following for their kind permission
to reproduce their photographs:

(Key: a-above; b-below/bottom; c-centre; f-far; l-left; r-right; t-top)

1 **Getty Images:** Samir Hussein / WireImage (b). 3 **Getty Images:** ullstein bild (r). 5 **Getty Images:** Chris Jackson - WPA Pool.
6 **Getty Images:** Mark Cuthbert / UK Press (bl). 7 **Corbis:** Gianni Dagli Orti (tl); The Gallery Collection (tr, cr); Tarker (cl).
Photoshot: World History Archive (bl). **SuperStock:** Classic Vision / age fotostock (br). 8 **Rex by Shutterstock:** Design Pics Inc (bl).
9 **akg-images:** arkivi (r). **Alamy Images:** Granger, NYC (tl). **Getty Images:** Tim Graham (bl). 10–11 **Corbis:** Jason Hawkes.
12 **Getty Images:** Topical Press Agency / Hulton Archive (bl). 13 **Getty Images:** Lisa Sheridan / Studio Lisa / Hulton Archive.
14–15 **Getty Images:** Popperfoto. 16–17 **Getty Images:** Tim Graham (bl). 18 **Getty Images:** POOL / Tim Graham Picture Library (b).
19 **Rex by Shutterstock.** 20 **Getty Images:** Fox Photos / Hulton Archive (b). 21 **Getty Images:** Central Press / Hulton Archive (b).
23 **Alamy Images:** V&A Images. 24–25 **Getty Images:** Arthur Edwards - WPA Pool. 26 **Getty Images:** Carl Court (b).
27 **Getty Images:** Anwar Hussein Collection / ROTA / WireImage (b). 28 **Getty Images:** Tim Graham (bl). 29 **Getty Images:** Martin
H. Simon-Pool (t). 30–31 **Corbis:** Gideon Mendel (b). 31 **Getty Images:** Lichfield (tr). 32 **Getty Images:** Indigo (b).
33 **Alamy Images:** Photopat (br). **Getty Images:** Indigo (t). 34 **Getty Images:** Max Mumby / Indigo (cla). 34–35 **Corbis:** Rolf
Vennenbernd / dpa. 36 **Corbis:** Duncan McGlynn / ActionPlus (cra); RoyalPress Nieboer / dpa (clb); WILL OLIVER / epa (crb).
Getty Images: Chris Jelf / Kensington Palace (bc); Max Mumby / Indigo (cb); Handout (bl). **iStockphoto.com:** EdStock (cla).
Rex by Shutterstock: (cb/Peter); David Hartley (bc/Savannah, br). 37 **Corbis:** Andy Rain / epa (tc); SDS / Newspix (bl).
Getty Images: Chris Jackson - WPA Pool (tl); Chris Jackson (cla); Max Mumby / Indigo (cra); David M. Benett (clb, cb).
Rex by Shutterstock: (cb/Louise, crb). 38 **Corbis:** Bettmann (bl). 39 **Getty Images:** Georges De Keerle (t). 40 **Rex by Shutterstock:**
Daily Mail (bl). 41 **Getty Images:** Fiona Hanson / AFP (t). 42 **Getty Images:** Mark Cuthbert / UK Press (b). 43 **Getty Images:** Hugo
Burnand / Pool (tr); Jonathan Brady - WPA Pool (b). 44 **Press Association Images:** Khan Tariq Mikkel / Polfoto (cr).
Rex by Shutterstock: Reginald Davis (b). 45 **Getty Images:** Chris Jackson (tr); Max Mumby / Indigo (bl). 46 **Getty Images:** Terry
Fincher / Princess Diana Archive (cr). 47 **Getty Images:** John Stillwell- WPA Pool (t). 48 **Getty Images:** Chris Jackson - WPA Pool (b).
49 **Corbis:** John Stillwell / PA Wire / epa (t). 50 **Getty Images:** Indigo (t). 51 **Getty Images:** Karwai Tang / WireImage (t).
52–53 **Getty Images:** Hugo Burnand / AFP. 54 **Getty Images:** Chris Jackson (t). 55 **Getty Images:** Chris Jackson (t); Handout (br).
56–57 **Getty Images:** Chris Jelf / Kensington Palace (b). 58–59 **Corbis:** Kerim Okten / epa.
60–61 **Getty Images:** Samir Hussein / WireImage.
Jacket images: Front: **Getty Images:** Chris Jackson - WPA Pool; Back: **Getty Images:** Chris Jackson tc, John Stillwell tr;
Rex by Shutterstock: Daily Mail tl; Spine: **Getty Images:** Chris Jackson - WPA Pool t

All other images © Dorling Kindersley
For further information see: www.dkimages.com

A WORLD OF IDEAS:
SEE ALL THERE IS TO KNOW

www.dk.com

Contents

Queen Elizabeth II

Her Majesty Queen Elizabeth II has been on the throne for more than 60 years. She is the longest reigning British monarch.

Like a queen in a fairy tale, Queen Elizabeth lives in palaces and castles. She even wears a crown, mainly for special occasions.

If you ever meet the Queen, you should greet her with a small curtsy or bow, or you may shake hands. Remember to call her "Your Majesty" when you're introduced!

Kings and Queens of Great Britain

For more than 1,500 years, kings and queens have reigned in Great Britain. The British throne is passed down through family lines, so most of these kings and queens were ancestors of our current queen, Elizabeth II.

Although Elizabeth II is called the Head of State, the laws of Great Britain are made by Parliament, which represents the people of the nation. This system is known as a constitutional monarchy.

Queen Elizabeth II

Some past kings and queens of Great Britain.

King Henry VIII

Queen Elizabeth I

King George III

Queen Victoria

King Edward VII

King George VI

The Crown Jewels

The Crown Jewels are a collection of royal ceremonial objects, such as crowns, sceptres and orbs. Many are priceless treasures, featuring the world's largest gems. The Crown Jewels are symbols of the British monarchy and are used for traditional ceremonies, including coronations and the annual State Opening of Parliament.

Since the 14th century, the Crown Jewels have been kept at the Tower of London, where they are guarded by the Yeoman Warders, also known as Beefeaters. Every year, millions of visitors see the Crown Jewels on public display.

The Sovereign's Orb is a gold sphere that is placed in the monarch's right hand during his or her coronation.

The Coronation Spoon and Ampulla
are used during coronations. Holy oil
is poured from the eagle-shaped
Ampulla into the spoon.

The Sceptre with the
Cross is a staff that is
decorated with diamonds.
It is used for coronations.

Queen Victoria's crown is a diamond headdress
that was used by Victoria after the death of her
husband, Prince Albert.

Windsor Castle

An official residence of the British Royal Family for more than 1,000 years, Windsor Castle sits on the banks of the River Thames at Windsor, a town just west of London. It stands in a former

royal hunting ground that is now a large park where deer still roam. Queen Elizabeth II often spends weekends at Windsor Castle and uses it to host official visits by overseas leaders. The public can tour much of the castle and its grounds.

An aerial view of Windsor Castle

Princess Elizabeth

Princess Elizabeth Alexandra Mary was born on 21 April 1926. Elizabeth and her younger sister, Margaret, spent their early childhood in a large house in London, where they had a governess to teach them. Elizabeth loved dogs and horses, a passion that has continued.

Elizabeth's life changed when her father was crowned King George VI. The family moved to the royal residence at Buckingham Palace and became role models for the nation. As the elder of the King's daughters, Elizabeth knew that she would one day become queen.

Princesses Elizabeth and Margaret joined a Girl Guide company at Buckingham Palace.

Princess Elizabeth with two of her corgi dogs in 1936.
The corgi is her favourite breed of dog.

Coronation of George VI

When Elizabeth's uncle, Edward VIII, decided he did not want to be king, Elizabeth's father became king instead, and took the name King George VI. This family picture was taken on the balcony of Buckingham Palace on the day of George VI's coronation in 1937.

Buckingham Palace

The Queen's official London residence is Buckingham Palace. The Royal Standard flag flies from the top of the palace when the Queen is at home. Of the palace's 775 rooms, the grandest are the State Rooms, used for official ceremonies and entertaining.

Buckingham Palace is the setting for many displays of royal pageantry, such as the famous Changing the Guard ceremony, when the palace guards change duties. The annual Trooping the Colour parade begins and ends at Buckingham Palace. Trooping the Colour marks the Queen's official birthday in June.

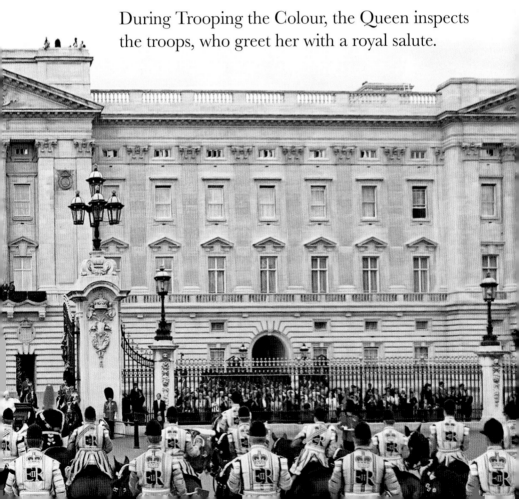

During Trooping the Colour, the Queen inspects the troops, who greet her with a royal salute.

Inside the Palace

About 50,000 people are invited to Buckingham Palace each year as guests at banquets, receptions and garden parties. In the summer, parts of the palace are open to the public. Visitors can see some of the State Rooms, such as the spectacular ballroom and Throne Room.

The palace ballroom was built in 1856. It was then the largest room in London.

The lavish Throne Room is used on formal occasions, such as coronations, jubilees and royal weddings.

World War II

When World War II started in 1939, Elizabeth was 13 years old. Despite the dangers of bombing in London, her parents, King George VI and Queen Elizabeth, remained at Buckingham Palace, where they could give support to people affected by the war. Meanwhile, Elizabeth and Margaret went to Windsor Castle, just outside London.

King George VI and Queen Elizabeth inspect bomb damage to Buckingham Palace in 1940.

The royal princesses wanted to help the war effort, too. The girls sewed and knitted for the troops. They also broadcast on the radio to keep up people's spirits. When she was old enough, Elizabeth joined the Auxiliary Territorial Service (ATS), where she served as a driver and mechanic. World War II ended in 1945, when Elizabeth was 19.

By the end of World War II, Princess Elizabeth was a Junior Commander in the ATS.

The Coronation

When her father, King George VI, died in 1952, Elizabeth was next in line to inherit the throne. On 2 June 1953, she was officially crowned Queen Elizabeth II. Following tradition, the Queen's Coronation took place at Westminster Abbey in London. The entire country celebrated the Coronation. Around the world, many more people watched the event on television. In her coronation speech, the Queen vowed, "Throughout all my life and with all my heart I shall strive to be worthy of your trust."

This Coronation photograph shows Queen Elizabeth II with the royal regalia from the Crown Jewels. Although she is wearing the Imperial State Crown, her official Coronation crown was the solid gold St Edward's Crown.

Parliament

The Queen is Head of State of Great Britain. One of her official duties in this role is the State Opening of Parliament, when she appears with the royal regalia. Members of both Houses of Parliament attend to hear the Queen read a speech outlining the government's priorities for the following parliamentary session. In more than 60 years as queen, Elizabeth II has only missed this event twice.

The Queen also meets regularly with the Prime Minister. Although she stays informed, she does not get involved in political decisions.

Queen Elizabeth II opens the new session of Parliament in 2015. With her are Prince Philip, Prince Charles and the Duchess of Cornwall.

Around Britain

Imagine if the Queen came to visit your school! Every year, members of the Royal Family go to about 3,000 public engagements around Britain.

The Queen participates in many official ceremonies. She also travels around the country, visiting schools,

Queen Elizabeth II lays a wreath during the annual Remembrance Sunday Service at the Cenotaph on Whitehall, London, in November 2015.

The Queen looks at a nativity collage made by schoolchildren at Southwark Cathedral, London, in December 2006.

hospitals, community centres, charities, businesses and other places.

Local bands and choirs often greet the Queen on her visits, and children present her with flowers. The Queen enjoys meeting people and finding out about what they do.

Travelling the World

The Queen is a popular international public figure. She is an ambassador for the nation, helping Great Britain's relationships with other countries.

Throughout her reign, she has travelled widely. Her first official trip as queen was a tour of the Commonwealth, countries around the world with links to the British monarchy. In all,

Queen Elizabeth II with Nceba Faku, the then mayor of Port Elizabeth, South Africa in March 1995

US President George W. Bush with the Queen on the South Lawn of the White House, Washington, D.C., in May 2007

the Queen has taken more than 260 trips to 116 countries.

The Queen's travel schedule is very busy, with up to 10 official engagements every day. She meets with many national leaders, but also likes to greet the public in the countries that she visits.

Royal Yacht, Britannia

From 1953 until 1997, the Royal Yacht *Britannia* sailed over a million miles, carrying the Royal Family all over the world, including across the Caribbean Sea, down the coast of Europe and around the Pacific islands. This elegant liner was the Royal Family's floating home for many official visits overseas.

The Royal Yacht *Britannia* docked at Cape Town during Queen Elizabeth II's trip to South Africa in 1995

The Royal Family also took holidays on the *Britannia*, when the crew helped to look after the royal children, organising games and treasure hunts on the ship. The children had chores to do, too, such as cleaning the life rafts.

The Queen on board *Britannia* in March 1972

Britannia ship is now docked in Edinburgh, where it is open to the public.

Royal Homes

Kensington Palace in London has been a royal residence since 1689. Queen Victoria was born there in 1819. Located in beautiful Kensington Gardens, the palace is now the London home of Princes William and Harry. Parts of the palace are open to the public.

Kensington Palace

Sandringham House

Sandringham is the royal residence near the Norfolk coast. The Royal Family usually gathers here for Christmas. During the summer, the Queen and Prince Philip often holiday at Balmoral Castle in the scenic Scottish Highlands.

Balmoral Castle

Horses

The Royal Family is known to love horses, both riding and going to the races. Over the years, the Queen has even owned her own racehorses and she enjoys watching them race – especially when they win!

Queen Elizabeth II in the parade ring at Newbury Racecourse in 2015

In 1976, her daughter, Princess Anne, competed in the equestrian events at the

Olympic Games. Anne's daughter, Zara Phillips, won a silver medal in the 2012 London Olympic Games as part of the British equestrian team. Princes William and Harry enjoy polo, a game played on horseback.

The Queen's granddaughter, Zara Phillips, was reigning Eventing World Champion until 2010. As well as winning a silver medal in the 2012 Olympics, she was part of the British team that won silver at the 2014 World Equestrian Games.

Royal Family Tree

This family tree shows the current Royal Family.

Charles

Anne

William

Harry

Peter

Zara

George

Charlotte

Savannah

Isla

Elizabeth

Philip

Andrew

Edward

Beatrice

Eugenie

Louise

James

Mia

—— Direct line to the throne

The Queen Mother

The Queen Mother is Queen Elizabeth's mum. In 1923, she married Prince Albert. When he was crowned King George VI in 1936, she took on the role of Queen. She supported the naturally shy King with her zest for life, and together they boosted the morale of the nation during World War II. When the King died in 1952, the Queen Mother gave her support to her daughter, Queen Elizabeth II.

The Queen Mother

The Queen Mother on her
90th birthday in 1990

The Queen Mother holds a special
place in the hearts of the British people.
On her 100th birthday, thousands of
people greeted her outside Buckingham
Palace. She also received the customary
telegram from the Queen for her
centenary. The Queen Mother died
in 2002 at the age of 101.

Prince Philip

Princess Elizabeth married Philip Mountbatten in 1947. To celebrate their marriage, Elizabeth's father, King George VI, gave Philip the title His Royal Highness The Duke of Edinburgh. Born in Greece, Philip was educated in England and became a British citizen. He was an officer in the Royal Navy when he married Elizabeth, but gave up his naval career when she became queen. The Queen and Prince Philip celebrated their 65th wedding anniversary in 2012.

Elizabeth and Philip on their wedding day, 20 November 1947

Elizabeth and Philip renewed their wedding vows on their Diamond Anniversary, celebrating 60 years of marriage

One of Prince Philip's contributions to British life is The Duke of Edinburgh's Awards. Since 1956, over 7 million young people in Britain and around the world have joined the scheme, which encourages participation in activities, such as physical fitness, volunteering and outdoor expeditions.

Charles, Prince of Wales

Born in 1948, Prince Charles is the Queen's eldest son, which means that he will be the next British monarch. He married Lady Diana Spencer in 1981 and they had two children, Prince William and Prince Harry. In 2005, Charles married Camilla Parker-Bowles.

Charles helps to raise over £100 million for charity each year. Through his own charity, the Prince's Trust, he aims to provide

Prince Charles

opportunities for young people in Britain. Since he founded it 40 years ago, the Prince's Trust has helped more than 825,000 people.

Charles with Camilla, after their wedding in 2005

Charles also supports environmental causes, enjoys painting and gardening and has written a children's book called *The Old Man of Lochnagar*.

Prince Charles with young people at the Surrey Cricket Club in January 2013

More Royals

Queen Elizabeth has three more children. Anne, Princess Royal, supports more than 300 organisations, including Save the Children and the International Olympic Committee. A champion rider, Anne competed in the 1976 Olympics. She has two grown-up children, Peter and Zara.

Anne, Princess Royal (*inset*) and on her horse Doublet, a gift from her mother, in 1972

Andrew, Duke of York, spent many years in the Royal Navy. As a member of the Royal Family, his main aim is to promote British business. He has two adult daughters, Beatrice and Eugenie.

Andrew, Duke of York

Edward, Earl of Wessex, worked in theatre and television production. He now represents his father's Duke of Edinburgh's Awards and the Wessex Youth Trust, which he founded with his

wife, Sophie, Countess of Wessex. They have two children, Louise and James.

The Earl and Countess of Wessex with their children

William, Duke of Cambridge

Born in 1982, William and his younger brother, Harry, grew up at Kensington Palace. They were devastated when their mother, Diana, died in a car crash in 1997.

Prince William and his mother, Diana, on his first official engagement in 1991

William met his future wife, Kate, while studying Geography at St Andrews University. After university, he trained to be an army officer. William then joined the Royal Air Force (RAF), where he became a Search and Rescue helicopter pilot, helping to rescue people in danger.

William at the controls of a Sea King helicopter during a training exercise at Holyhead Mountain in 2011

In 2015, William began work as a helicopter pilot with the East Anglian Air Ambulance (EAAA), where he is given time off for royal duties. He donates his salary to charity.

Prince Harry

Prince Henry of Wales (Harry) was born in 1984. After finishing his A-levels, Harry spent a gap year travelling to Australia, Argentina and Africa. While in Africa, he filmed a documentary about orphans in Lesotho. This inspired Harry to co-found a charity to help children in Lesotho.

Prince Harry with children in Lesotho, Africa, in 2014. These children study in a school built by Sentebale, Harry's African charity.

Harry at Camp Bastion, Afghanistan, in 2012

The charity is called Sentebale, which means "forget me not", in honour of his mother, Diana.

Harry spent 10 years as a pilot in the Army Air Corps, rising to the rank of Captain. In 2014, he organised the first Invictus Games, a sporting competition for injured military staff. He has also trekked to the South Pole to raise awareness of the issue.

Catherine, Duchess of Cambridge

Catherine (Kate) Middleton met Prince William in 2001 at St Andrews University in Scotland, where she studied History of Art. Born in 1982, Kate worked for her family's online party business after university, and also for a fashion company.

Catherine, Duchess of Cambridge, at Queen Elizabeth II's Diamond Jubilee celebrations in 2012

The Duchess meeting children in London in November 2015 as part of her charity work on mental health

Kate has certainly added glamour to the Royal Family. She is also known to be sporty and down-to-earth with a good sense of humour. Since marrying William, Kate has thrown herself into her royal duties, especially charities. She has said, "I really hope I can make a difference, even in the smallest way."

Royal Wedding

Prince William and Kate Middleton married on 29 April 2011, when the Queen gave them the titles Duke and Duchess of Cambridge. More than 1,900 guests attended the wedding. The day was declared a national holiday in the UK, while around the world millions more watched the wedding on TV and online. The Duke and Duchess of Cambridge will one day become King William and Queen Catherine.

Prince George

Prince George, great-grandchild of Queen Elizabeth II, was born in 2013. Formally known as His Royal Highness Prince George of Cambridge, this little boy is third in line to the throne after his

Prince George enjoys the annual Trooping the Colour ceremony with his father in 2015.

grandfather, the Prince of Wales, and his father, the Duke of Cambridge. George's birth was the first royal announcement by email. The news was then tweeted around the world – another first.

When he was eight months old, baby George joined his parents on a royal visit to Australia and New Zealand where he

George heads home with his parents after his first royal tour to Australia in 2014.

proved to be very popular. A lively, playful boy, George had his first day at a local nursery in January 2016.

Prince George on his first day of nursery school in 2016

Princess Charlotte

When Her Royal Highness Princess
Charlotte of Cambridge was born in
2015, she received many letters and cards
of welcome, especially from children.
Girls named Charlotte wrote to show
their delight at the Princess' name. Some

children also wrote to advise Prince George on how to be a good brother.

The Duke and Duchess of Cambridge and their children now live mostly at Anmer Hall on the Queen's Sandringham Estate in Norfolk with Lupo, the family dog. Their London residence is at Kensington Palace.

The Duke and Duchess of Cambridge with their children, Prince George and Princess Charlotte

Diamond Jubilee

In 2012, Queen Elizabeth II completed 60 years on the throne. People around the country celebrated her Diamond Jubilee with street parties, picnics and other events. Seen here is the spectacular Diamond Jubilee pageant that featured more than 1,000 boats sailing down the River Thames in London.

Timeline for Queen Elizabeth II

1926
The future
Queen Elizabeth II
is born.

1952
King George VI
dies. Elizabeth
becomes Queen.

1964
Edward is bor

1950
Anne is born.

1960
Andrew is born.

1948
Charles is born.
He is next in line
to the throne after
Elizabeth.

1947
Elizabeth marries
Philip Mountbatten.

1982
William is born.
He is second in
line to the throne.

2002
Elizabeth celebrates
her Golden Jubilee.
She completes 50
years on the throne.

2013
George is born. He is
third in line to the throne.

2016
Elizabeth
celebrates her
90th birthday.

2015
Charlotte is born.

1984
Harry is born.

2012
Diamond Jubilee marks 60
years of Queen Elizabeth II
on the throne.

1977
Silver Jubilee. The
Queen celebrates
25 years on the throne.

Royal Facts

Every Christmas, the Queen appears on TV to give her annual message to the people of the UK.

The British Monarchy has an official website, YouTube channel, Twitter handle, Flickr account and Facebook page.

Since she became Queen, Elizabeth has posed for 129 portraits, including a hologram portrait.

The Queen celebrates two birthdays. Her real birthday is on 21 April, while her official birthday is celebrated in June.

The "Elizabeth Line" is a new railway line in London, named after the Queen.

The Queen sends messages congratulating British people on their 100th birthday and 60th wedding anniversary.

Queen Victoria was the only other British monarch to celebrate a Diamond Jubilee, marking 60 years on the throne.

During her reign, the Queen has replied to more than 3 million items of correspondence.

Glossary

ancestor
family from the past, such as great-grandparents

centenary
celebration marking one hundred years

coronation
official crowning ceremony

head of state
highest or main representative of a country

monarch
king or queen

pageantry
grand display, often of a ceremony

parliament
group of people who make the laws in a country

regalia
symbols of royalty

reign
time during which a monarch is on the throne

residence
home